D0764252

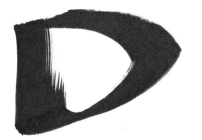

Formas: Cuadrados
Shapes: Squares

Esther Sarfatti

Rourke
Publishing LLC
Vero Beach, Florida 32964

www.rourkepublishing.com

PHOTO CREDITS: © Jim Lopes: page 5; © Radu Razvan: page 7; © Sean Locke and Nicholas Belton: page 9; © Andrew Johnson: page 11; © M. Eric Honeycutt: page 13; © Don Joski: page 15; © Vorakorn Tuvajitt: page 17; © Rebecca Paul: page 19; © Tomasz Tulik: page 21; © Flavia Bottazzini: page 23.

Editor: Robert Stengard-Olliges

Cover design by Nicola Stratford.

Library of Congress Cataloging-in-Publication Data

Sarfatti, Esther.
  [Shapes. Squares. Spanish]
  Formas. Cuadrados / Esther Sarfatti.
    p. cm. -- (Conceptos)
  ISBN 978-1-60044-753-2
  1. Square--Juvenile literature. 2. Shapes--Juvenile literature. I. Title. II. Title: Cuadrados.
  QA482.S35918 2008
  516'.154--dc22
                    2007022565

Printed in the USA

CG/CG

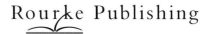

Rourke Publishing

www.rourkepublishing.com – rourke@rourkepublishing.com
Post Office Box 3328, Vero Beach, FL 32964

Esto es un cuadrado.
This is a square.

Hay cuadrados por todas partes.

Squares are everywhere.

5

Estas galletas son cuadradas.

These crackers are square.

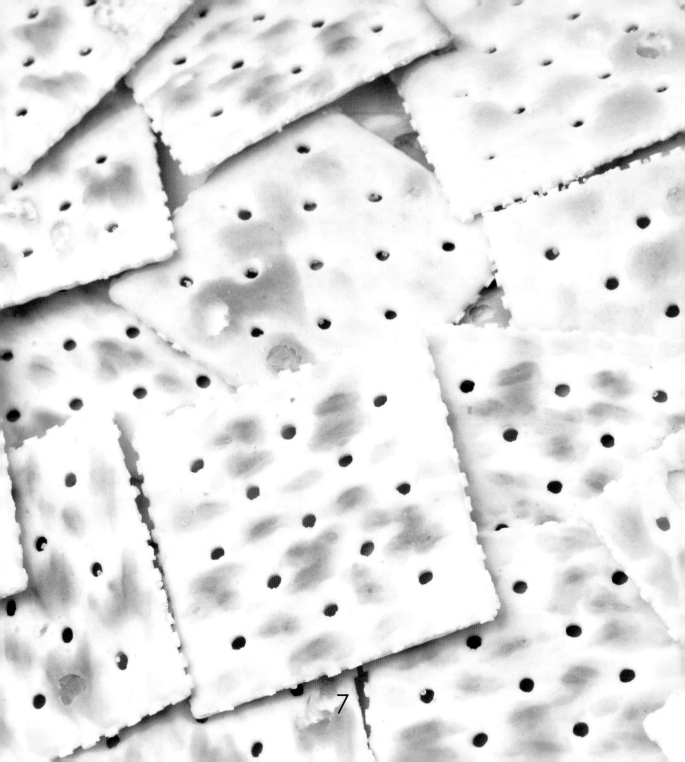
7

Esta foto es cuadrada.

This picture is square.

Este rompecabezas
es cuadrado.

This puzzle is square.

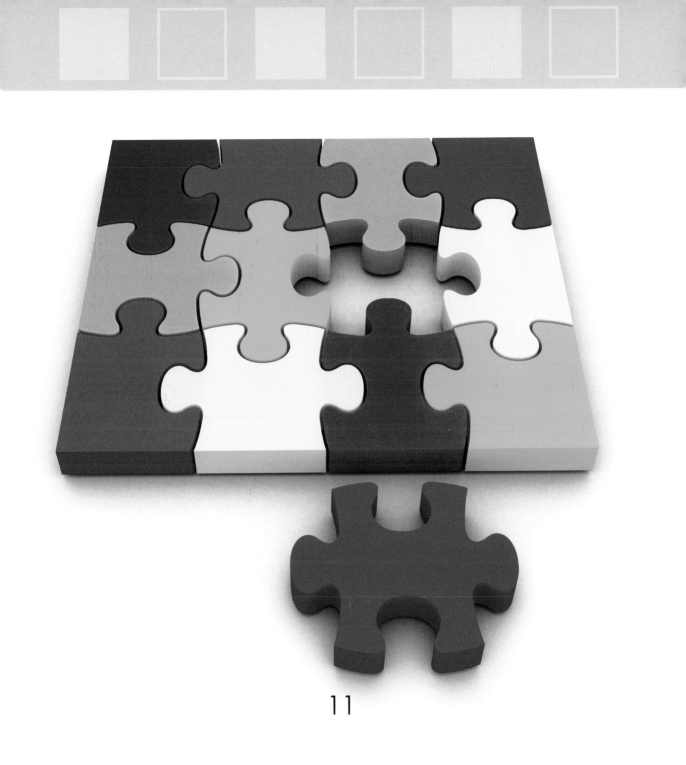

11

Estas baldosas son cuadradas.

These tiles are squares.

13

Estos cojines son cuadrados.

These pillows are squares.

Estos dulces son cuadrados.

These brownies are squares.

Este reloj es un cuadrado.

This clock is a square.

19

Estos cubitos de hielo
son cuadrados.

These ice cubes are squares.

21

Hay cuadrados por
todas partes.
¿Puedes encontrar
los cuadrados?

Squares are everywhere.
Can you find the squares?

Índice

Index

Lecturas adicionales / Further Reading

Leake, Diyan. *Finding Shapes: Squares*. Heinemann, 2005.

Olson, Nathan. *Squares Around Town*. A+ Books, 2007.

Páginas Web recomendadas / Recommended Websites

www.enchantedlearning.com/themes/shapes.shtml

Acerca de la autora / About the Author

Esther Sarfatti lleva más de 15 años trabajando con libros infantiles como editora y traductora. Ésta es su primera serie como autora. Nacida en Brooklyn, Nueva York, donde creció en una familia trilingüe, Esther vive actualmente en Madrid, España, con su esposo y su hijo.

Esther Sarfatti has worked with children's books for over 15 years as an editor and translator. This is her first series as an author. Born in Brooklyn, New York, and brought up in a trilingual home, Esther currently lives with her husband and son in Madrid, Spain.